KU-410-086

Puffin Books

The Young Puffin Quiz Book

From the author of the highly popular *Copycat*, *Copyparty* and *Copycard* comes this carefully graded quiz book for young children.

Starting with very simple questions which draw mainly on children's observation of their immediate environment, the questions gradually become more difficult, requiring a wider general knowledge. The lively and amusing illustrations will help the youngest child with the most limited experience to find the right answers and will certainly stimulate lots of new questions and ideas.

Tested (and approved) by primary-school pupils, this book will be a great source of fun and interest, and will keep young children absorbed for many happy hours.

Acknowledgements

Sally Kilroy and Puffin Books would like to thank
Clive Butler and the children of Darell Primary
School in Richmond, Surrey, for their enthusiastic
assistance in preparing this book for publication.

Puffin Books, Penguin Books Ltd, Harmondsworth, Middlesex, England
Viking Penguin Inc., 40 West 23rd Street, New York, New York 10010, U.S.A.
Penguin Books Australia Ltd, Ringwood, Victoria, Australia
Penguin Books Canada Ltd, 2801 John Street, Markham, Ontario, Canada L3R 1B4
Penguin Books (N.Z.) Ltd, 182–190 Wairau Road, Auckland 10, New Zealand

First published 1982
Reprinted 1983, 1984, 1987

Text and illustrations copyright © Sally Kilroy, 1982
All rights reserved

Made and printed in Great Britain by
Hazell Watson & Viney Limited,
Member of the BPCC Group,
Aylesbury, Bucks
Composition in Helvetica Medium by Filmtype Services Limited,
Scarborough, North Yorkshire.

Except in the United States of America, this book is sold subject
to the condition that it shall not, by way of trade or otherwise, be lent,
re-sold, hired out, or otherwise circulated without the
publisher's prior consent in any form of binding or cover other than
that in which it is published and without a similar condition
including this condition being imposed on the subsequent purchaser

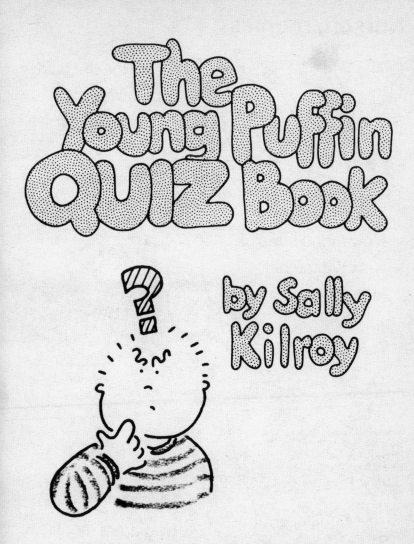

The Young Puffin QUIZ Book

by Sally Kilroy

For Sarah and Rupert

Puffin Books

Nursery rhymes

Who did the dish run away with?

a) the shovel
b) a banana
c) the spoon

How many bags of wool did the black sheep have?

a) three
b) four
c) five

What frightened Miss Muffet?

a) a hairy monster
b) a spider
c) a bat

What did Jack Horner
pull out of the pie?

a) a plum
b) a blackbird
c) a marble

Who had a great fall
from a wall?

a) Coco the clown
b) a clumsy man
c) Humpty Dumpty

Who lived in a shoe?

a) Little Bo Peep
b) Alice in Wonderland
c) an old woman

Food

Which animal does
ham come from?

a) an elephant
b) a sheep
c) a pig

Where do bananas grow?

a) underground
b) on trees
c) on bushes

Which vegetable
makes your eyes water
when you peel it?

a) a potato
b) an onion
c) a tomato

Where does spaghetti
come from?

a) France
b) Spain
c) Italy

What is the best time of
year for fresh strawberries?

a) summer
b) spring
c) winter

What is candyfloss
made from?

a) treacle
b) jam
c) sugar

The weather

What is a short burst
of rain called?

a) snow   b) a shower
   c) a storm

What goes up when
the rain comes down?

a) a sunhat
b) an umbrella
c) a parachute

What is snow made of?

a) water
b) white paint
c) cotton wool

Where does the sun rise?

a) in the east   b) in the north

c) in the west

What do we call
a very strong wind?

a) a gale

b) a storm

c) a breeze

OOPS!

What colour is the sky
when it's going to rain?

a) blue

b) grey

c) pink

At the beach

Look at the picture
and answer the questions.

What is pinching the
boy's foot?

a) an octopus
b) a jellyfish
c) a crab

What bird are you
most likely to see
at the seaside?

a) a bluetit
b) a sparrow
c) a seagull

What is a lighthouse for?

a) for people to see
   the view from
b) to send signals
   inland
c) to warn ships
   where land is

What do ships lower to
keep them in one place?

a) a rope
b) an old boot
c) an anchor

What pushes a sailing boat along?

a) the wind
b) an engine
c) oars

What gets wetter as you get drier?

a) the sea
b) a towel
c) the sun

What is a two-piece
swimsuit called?

a) a tank top

b) a trouser suit

c) a bikini

Who blows a spout
of water?

a) a seal

b) a whale

c) a porpoise

What is this
person doing?

a) sailing

b) surfing

c) water-skiing

What can you wear
to see under water?
a) glasses
b) binoculars
c) a mask

What is a wreck?
a) an old cannon
b) a sunken ship
c) a fish tank

What is this?
a) a jellyfish
b) a shark
c) an octopus

Fairy tales

How many dwarfs lived with Snow White?

   a) five
   b) nine
   c) seven

What did the ugly duckling turn into?

a) a chicken
b) a crocodile
c) a swan

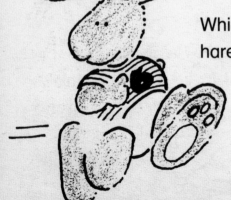

Which animal did the hare have a race with?

   a) a fox
   b) a tortoise
   c) a duck

Who was always being nasty to Cinderella?

a) Buttons
b) the Fairy Godmother
c) the Ugly Sisters

TICK! TOCK!

What did the crocodile have in his stomach in the story of Peter Pan?

a) a kettle
b) a clock
c) a mouse

HUBBLE!
BUBBLE!

What does a witch cook up her spells in?

a) a bucket
b) a bowl
c) a cauldron

At school

What do you use to
stick things together?

a) ink
b) custard
c) glue

What is this?

a) a map
b) a diary
c) a calendar

What is a skeleton made of?

a) wood b) bone c) metal

What is black when clean and white when dirty?

a) a zebra crossing
b) a panda
c) a blackboard

What is this?

a) a light
b) a puppet
c) a mobile

What colour do you get if you mix blue and red?

a) green   b) purple   c) orange

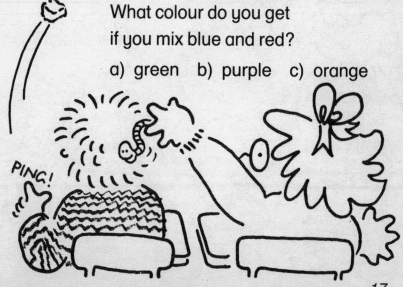

Clothes

Look at the pictures and answer the questions.

What do you wear to
keep your neck warm?

a) a woolly hat
b) a scarf
c) warm boots

What is the child with
glasses wearing?

a) jeans
b) a dress
c) dungarees

What fastens sandals?

a) laces
b) poppers
c) buckles

What should you wear
on your feet when you
jump in puddles?

a) gym shoes
b) bedroom slippers
c) wellingtons

What do we call
a jumper with buttons
down the front?

a) a polo neck
b) a sweater
c) a cardigan

What is this woolly
hat called?

a) a pom-pom hat
b) a balaclava
c) a beret

Numbers

How many letters are there in the alphabet?

a) thirty-two
b) twenty-six
c) forty

How many legs does a spider have?

a) four
b) eight
c) six

EEK!

FRESH FARM EGGS

How many eggs do you get in a box?

a) nine
b) eight
c) six

How many ten pence pieces
are there in a pound?
a) ten
b) twenty
c) five

How many months
are there in a year?
a) twenty-four
b) six
c) twelve

How many babies make a set of triplets?

a) six   b) three   c) nine

How many letters
are there in the name
ELIZABETH?

a) seven
b) nine
c) eleven

How many
make a pair?

a) two
b) four
c) six

How many holes
are there on a
telephone dial?

a) nine
b) twenty
c) ten

How many cards are
there in a pack?

a) thirty
b) fifty-two
c) twenty-seven

How many days are
there in a week?

a) seven
b) fourteen
c) ten

How many years are
there in a century?

a) one million
b) ten
c) one hundred

Shopping

What does the butcher sell?

a) potatoes

b) meat

c) pots and pans

What would you get
from a bank?

a) plants

b) shoes

c) money

Where can you
borrow books?

a) the library

b) the newsagent

c) the baker

What do you push your shopping round in at a supermarket?

a) a trailer
b) a trolley
c) a truck

In which shop can you buy medicines?

a) the chemist
b) the greengrocer
c) the sports shop

What are things weighed on?

a) a counter
b) a calculator
c) a pair of scales

Around the house

What do we call
the pouring part
of a teapot?

a) the funnel
b) the handle
c) the spout

What do you need to
unlock a front door?

a) a bell
b) a key
c) a knocker

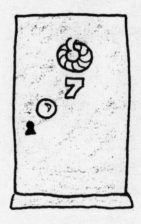

What do you use to
sweep up dust?

a) a mop and bucket
b) a bucket and spade
c) a dustpan and brush

What do you rest
your head on
when you sleep?

a) the floor
b) the bedhead
c) a pillow

What do we call
the doors that close
over windows?

a) curtains
b) French windows
c) shutters

What do you see if you
look in a mirror?

a) a cat
b) the person next door
c) yourself

Look at the pictures and answer
the questions.

What do you need
to climb up to
reach the roof?

a) a stool
b) a staircase
c) a ladder

What do you cut
the grass with?

a) an electric shaver
b) a vacuum cleaner
c) a lawn mower

Which of these is
not a vegetable?

a) a potato
b) a pear
c) a parsnip

What would you use to
water the flowers?

a) a bucket
b) a watering-can
c) a teapot

How many wheels does
a wheelbarrow have?

a) three
b) one
c) two

What would you clip
the hedge with?

a) a pair of scissors
b) a knife
c) a pair of shears

EEK!

Famous people and places

Where does the Queen live?

a) Longleat
b) Buckingham Palace
c) the British Museum

What do we call the person at the head of the government?

a) the President
b) the Queen
c) the Prime Minister

Where are the Crown Jewels kept?

a) the Tower of London
b) in the Queen's jewel box
c) in a bank

What is this man called?

a) a sailor
b) a beefeater
c) a soldier

Where is money made?

a) the Royal Mint
b) the Royal Toffee
c) the Royal Coin Factory

What did Guy Fawkes try to do?

a) light a bonfire
b) steal some fireworks
c) blow up Parliament

Wild animals

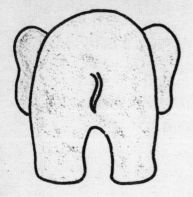

Who carries a trunk about all day?

a) a porter
b) someone on holiday
c) an elephant

What do we call the fur around a lion's head?

a) a scarf
b) a mane
c) a beard

What colour is a polar bear?

a) grey
b) brown
c) white

Which animal carries
her baby in a pouch?

a) an anteater
b) a bear
c) a kangaroo

_____

Which animal has black and white stripes?

a) a tiger   b) a zebra   c) a cow

Which big fish shows its fin above water?

a) a goldfish   b) a shark   c) a cod

Which big cat
has spots?

a) a leopard
b) a tiger
c) a puma

Where do penguins come from?

a) the North Pole
b) Africa
c) the South Pole

When did the first
dinosaurs live?

a) 1,000 years ago
b) 1,000,000 years ago
c) 200,000,000 years ago

Name the animal
with one hump
on his back.

a) a gorilla
b) a rhinoceros
c) a camel

CHOMP!

What do pandas eat?

a) baked beans
b) bamboo
c) bananas

What do hippopotamuses
like doing best?

a) climbing trees
b) playing tennis
c) swimming

Jobs

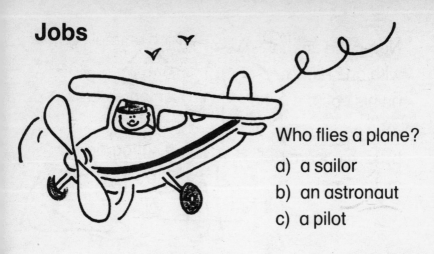

Who flies a plane?

a) a sailor
b) an astronaut
c) a pilot

Who gets the sack as soon
as he starts work?

a) a doctor
b) a postman
c) a roadsweeper

What do we call a person who works underwater?

a) a miner   b) a waterbaby   c) a diver

Who would you find at
Scotland Yard?

a) a lot of chickens
b) a Scotsman
c) the police

Who paints pictures?

a) a decorator
b) an artist
c) an author

Who makes things in wood?

a) an electrician
b) a woodman
c) a carpenter

Buildings

What is this called?

a) a balcony
b) a verandah
c) a patio

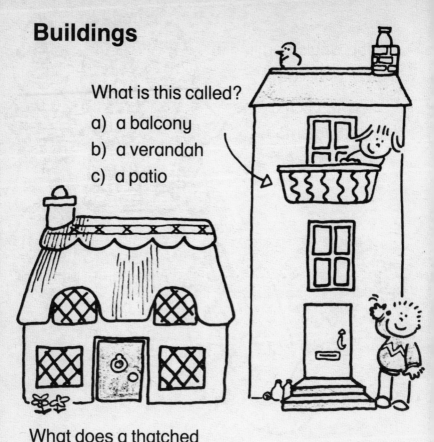

What does a thatched
cottage have on the roof?

a) straw
b) tiles
c) slates

What do we call the machine that
knocks buildings down?

a) a steam roller   b) a juggernaut   c) a bulldozer

What is this part of a
church called?

a) the chimney
b) the spire
c) the roof

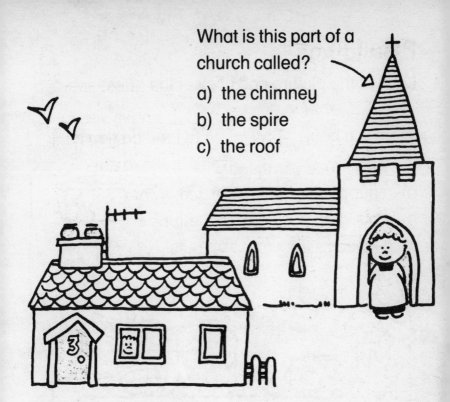

What is a bungalow?

a) a wooden house
b) a house that stands
   on its own
c) a house with no
   upstairs

Where are cars made?

a) factories
b) garages
c) offices

Pets

Look at the picture and answer the questions.

What is a baby
cat called?

a) a puppy
b) a budgie
c) a kitten

What food do you think
rabbits like to eat?

a) ice-cream
b) lettuce
c) nuts

What sort of dog is in this picture?

a) a bulldog
b) a poodle
c) a labrador

What does a tadpole become?

a) a snake
b) a crocodile
c) a frog

Which pet carries its house on its back?

a) a pony
b) a goldfish
c) a tortoise

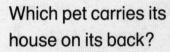

WOOF!

Who would you see if your pet became ill?

a) the doctor
b) the dentist
c) the vet

In the countryside

Look at the picture
and answer the questions.

What is an evergreen tree?

a) a tree with a green trunk
b) a tree that loses its
   leaves in winter
c) a tree that keeps its
   leaves all year

What do you eat
that has one middle
and two outsides?

a) a bun
b) a sandwich
c) an apple

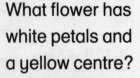

What flower has
white petals and
a yellow centre?

a) a foxglove
b) a daffodil
c) a daisy

Where do you sleep when
you go camping?

a) in a hotel
b) under a log
c) in a tent

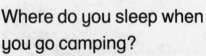

What keeps drinks hot?

a) a teapot

b) a jug

c) a Thermos flask

What animal rolls into a spiky ball to protect itself?

a) a squirrel

b) a hedgehog

c) a dormouse

Which bird comes
out at night?
a) the robin
b) the blackbird
c) the owl

What has six legs,
four ears and a tail?
a) a spider
b) a donkey and cart
c) a man on a horse

What will a caterpillar turn into?

a) a snake   b) a bee   c) a butterfly

What has a white
fluffy tail?

a) a hedgehog
b) a rabbit
c) a squirrel

Pick out the bird's footprints.

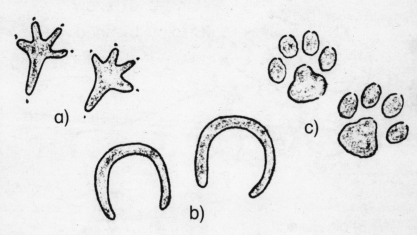

a)

b)

c)

How does a bat sleep?

a) lying on a branch
b) hanging upside down
c) curled up in leaves

People and places

What is a Red Indian's
tent called?

a) a totem pole
b) a squaw
c) a wigwam

What would be all around you in the desert?

a) snow
b) sand
c) water

What do we call
a piece of land completely
surrounded by water?

a) a bay
b) a peninsula
c) an island

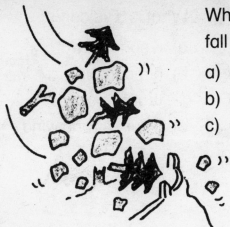

What do we call a big fall of rocks?

a) an earthquake
b) an avalanche
c) a landslide

Where do oranges grow?
a) Spain
b) Iceland
c) Norway

What would an Indian woman wear?

a) a grass skirt
b) a sari
c) a kilt

What is a volcano?

a) a spout of water
b) a mountain
   that explodes
c) a very strong wind

Who used to live in igloos?

a) Germans
b) Indians
c) Eskimos

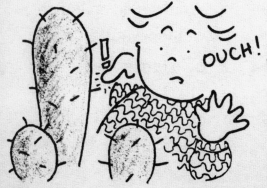

OUCH!

Where do cactuses grow wild?

a) under the sea
b) in the desert
c) in the snow

What is the top of a
mountain called?

a) the ceiling
b) the crust
c) the summit

Where do parrots
come from?

a) the sea
b) the mountains
c) the jungle

Where would you find an iceberg?

a) in a hot country   b) in a desert
c) in cold water

Sport

Who wears gloves?

a) gymnasts   b) footballers   c) boxers

What do you play
tennis with?

a) a bat
b) a racket
c) a stick

What do you wear
on your feet
at an ice-rink?

a) thick socks
b) gym shoes
c) skates

What is this person riding?

a) a scooter
b) a skateboard
c) a tin tray

Who rides race horses?
a) a bookie
b) a starter
c) a jockey

How many people are there in a football team?

a) nine   b) seventeen   c) eleven

What game would you
play with these pieces?

a) draughts
b) ludo
c) chess

What do you use instead
of a ball in badminton?

a) a stick
b) a wicket
c) a shuttlecock

What sport is this
person playing?

a) cricket
b) hockey
c) rounders

What is this
person doing?

a) flying a plane
b) flying a kite
c) hang-gliding

Which game uses a
ball shaped like this?

a) football
b) rugby
c) cricket

What is a float used for in fishing?

a) to attract the fish
b) to show when you have
   caught a fish
c) to keep boats away

On the farm

Look at the picture and answer the questions.

What is the farmer driving?

a) a lorry
b) a jeep
c) a tractor

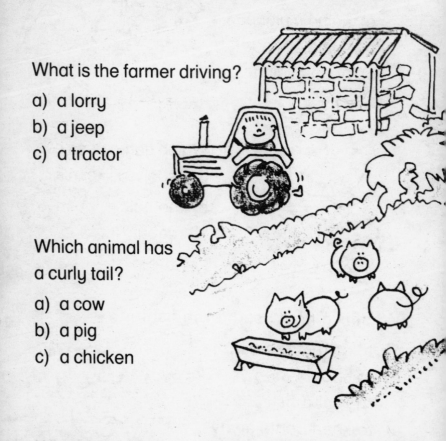

Which animal has a curly tail?

a) a cow
b) a pig
c) a chicken

Where does milk come from?

a) a machine
b) trees
c) cows

Which animal's coat would make a woolly jumper?

a) a kangaroo
b) a gorilla
c) a sheep

Who helps a shepherd
to round up sheep?

a) a cat

b) a sheepdog

c) a horse

Where does a farmer
keep hay in winter?

a) under his hat

b) in his house

c) in a barn

What is a baby
sheep called?

a) a piglet
b) a calf
c) a lamb

What is cheese
made from?

a) apples
b) milk
c) sausages

What do some farmers
use to keep birds
from their crops?

a) a cat
b) a wild mouse
c) a scarecrow

What do we call
a male cow?

a) a ram
b) a bull
c) a boar

What do we call
the machine that
gathers corn?

a) a plough
b) a scythe
c) a combine harvester

What is the name for the
red part of a cock's head?

a) a forelock
b) a comb
c) a fringe

Transport

What do we call a cycle
with three wheels?

a) a tandem
b) a tricycle
c) a triangle

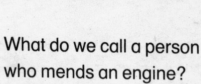

What do we call a person
who mends an engine?

a) a mechanic
b) a plumber
c) a gardener

What makes
new roads flat?

a) a big lorry
b) a dumper truck
c) a steam roller

What do we call the person
in charge of a ship?

a) the pilot
b) the captain
c) the commander

What colour are traffic
lights from top to bottom?

a) red, green, amber
b) amber, red, green
c) red, amber, green

What do you call a
flat tyre?

a) a puncture
b) a bust-up
c) a short cut

**What lifts
heavy things?**

a) a crane
b) a tanker
c) a lorry

**What do you put in a
car to make it go?**

a) peanuts
b) water
c) petrol

What is this?

a) a helicopter   b) a Hoover   c) a hovercraft

Who checks your ticket on a train?

a) a porter
b) a ticket collector
c) a guard

What do we call a boat
that carries people
and their cars?

a) a cargo boat
b) a liner
c) a ferry

What does this road
sign mean?

a) slippery road
b) road narrows
c) children crossing

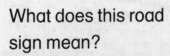

Music

What is this instrument?

a) a saxophone
b) a trumpet
c) a horn

What is a choir?

a) a football crowd
b) a school band
c) a group of singers

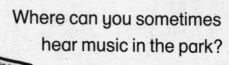

Where can you sometimes hear music in the park?

a) at the ice-cream kiosk
b) on the bowling green
c) at a bandstand

What do we call the
person who keeps the
orchestra in time?

a) the drummer
b) the conductor
c) the pianist

What are these?

a) notes
b) letters
c) blobs

What is a busker?

a) a person who sells
   instruments
b) a person who plays
   a drum
c) a pavement musician

Special days

What date is
Christmas Day?

a) December 23rd
b) December 31st
c) December 25th

What day is
February 14th?

a) Easter Day
b) St Valentine's Day
c) Bank holiday

Who owns a reindeer
with a red nose?

a) Coco the clown
b) Father Christmas
c) Mother Goose

What do people give to each other at Easter?

a) fish and chips
b) bacon and eggs
c) Easter eggs

Who are supposed to come out on the night of October 31st?

a) fairies
b) ghosts
c) witches

What is the proper name for Pancake Day?

a) Palm Sunday
b) Good Friday
c) Shrove Tuesday

Law and order

Where are criminals
locked up?

a) in the bathroom
b) in jail
c) at school

Who gives you a ticket for
parking in the wrong place?

a) a traffic warden
b) a ticket collector
c) a bus conductor

What colour is the flashing
light on a police car?

a) red
b) yellow
c) blue

What does a judge
wear on his head?

a) a bowler hat
b) a wig
c) a cap

What do we call a
person who steals?

a) a waiter
b) a cashier
c) a burglar

What is a policeman's
stick called?

a) a truncheon
b) a bat
c) a pogo stick

Fun and games

Coco's trousers are always falling down. What should he get to hold them up?

a) a hammer and nails
b) glue
c) braces

Who are these people?

a) Meg and Mog
b) Punch and Judy
c) Tom and Jerry

What kind of cars crash into each other at funfairs?

a) old bangers   b) roller coasters
c) bumper cars

What do we call a person
who does magic tricks?

a) a trickster
b) a wizard
c) a magician

What are these people?

a) clowns
b) acrobats
c) jugglers

What is the name of the special swing that circus people use?

a) a see-saw
b) a trampoline
c) a trapeze

WHEE!

What do we call a circus tent?

a) a wigwam   b) a big top

c) a round house

Who performs in a ballet?

a) dancers

b) acrobats

c) clowns

Space

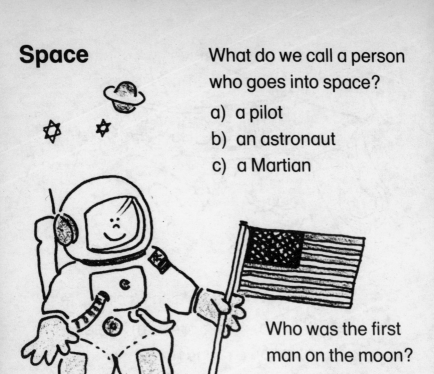

What do we call a person who goes into space?

a) a pilot
b) an astronaut
c) a Martian

Who was the first man on the moon?

a) Tom Brown
b) Neil Armstrong
c) Charlie Chaplin

How far is the sun from Earth?

a) 17 million miles
b) 52 million miles
c) 93 million miles

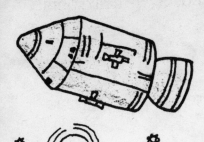

Which part of a rocket do astronauts fly in?

a) the engine room
b) the command module
c) mission control

What sends pictures from space?

a) television
b) telescopes
c) satellites

What do we call a spacecraft that can be used again?

a) a jumbo jet
b) skylab
c) a space shuttle

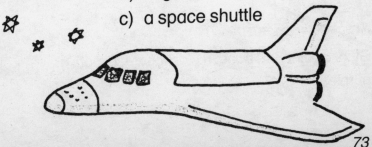

Answers

Nursery rhymes (pages 4–5)

The spoon, three, a spider, a plum, Humpty Dumpty, an old woman

Food (pages 6–7)

A pig, on trees, an onion, Italy, summer, sugar

Weather (pages 8–9)

A shower, an umbrella, water, in the east, a gale, grey

At the beach (pages 10–13)

A crab, a seagull, to warn ships where land is, an anchor, the wind, a towel

A bikini, a whale, water-skiing, a mask, a sunken ship, an octopus

Fairy tales (pages 14–15)

Seven, a swan, a tortoise, the Ugly Sisters, a clock, a cauldron

At school (pages 16–17)

Glue, a calendar, bone, a blackboard, a mobile, purple

Clothes (pages 18–19)

A scarf, dungarees, buckles, a cardigan, wellingtons, a balaclava

Numbers (pages 20–23)

Twenty-six, eight, six, ten, twelve, three

Nine, two, ten, fifty-two, seven, one hundred

Shopping (pages 24–25)

Meat, money, the library, a trolley, the chemist, a pair of scales

Around the house (pages 26–29)

The spout, a key, a dustpan and brush, a pillow, shutters, yourself

A lawn mower, a ladder, a pear, a watering can, one, a pair of shears

Famous people and places (pages 30–31)

Buckingham Palace, the Prime Minister, the Tower of London, a beefeater, the Royal Mint, blow up Parliament

Wild animals (pages 32–35)

An elephant, a mane, white, a kangaroo, a zebra, a shark

A leopard, the South Pole, 200,000,000 years ago, a camel, bamboo, swimming

Jobs (pages 36–37)

A pilot, a postman, a diver, the police, an artist, a carpenter

Buildings (pages 38–39)

A balcony, straw, a bulldozer, the spire, a house with no upstairs, factories

Pets (pages 40–41)

A kitten, lettuce, a poodle, a frog, a tortoise, the vet

In the countryside (pages 42–45)

A tree that keeps its leaves all year, a sandwich, a daisy, in a tent, a Thermos flask, a hedgehog

The owl, a man on a horse, a butterfly, a rabbit, footprints (a), hanging upside down

People and places (pages 46–49)

A wigwam, sand, an island, a landslide, Spain, a sari

A mountain that explodes, Eskimos, in the desert, the summit, the jungle, in cold water

Sport (pages 50–53)

Boxers, a racket, skates, a skateboard, a jockey, eleven

Chess, a shuttlecock, hockey, hang-gliding, rugby, to show when you have caught a fish

On the farm (pages 54–57)

A tractor, a pig, cows, a sheep, a sheepdog, in a barn

A lamb, milk, a scarecrow, a bull, a combine harvester, a comb

Transport (pages 58–61)

A tricycle, a mechanic, a steam roller, the captain, red/amber/green, a puncture

A crane, petrol, a hovercraft, a ticket collector, a ferry, road narrows

Music (pages 62–63)

A saxophone, a group of singers, at a bandstand, the conductor, notes, a pavement musician

Special days (pages 64–65)

December 25th, St Valentine's Day, Father Christmas, Easter eggs, witches, Shrove Tuesday

Law and order (pages 66–67)

In jail, a traffic warden, blue, a wig, a burglar, a truncheon

Fun and games (pages 68–71)

Braces, Punch and Judy, bumper cars, a magician

Acrobats, a trapeze, a big top, dancers

Space (pages 72–73)

An astronaut, Neil Armstrong, 93 million miles, the command module, satellites, a space shuttle

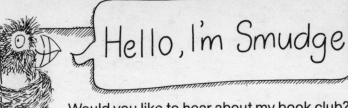

Hello, I'm Smudge

Would you like to hear about my book club?

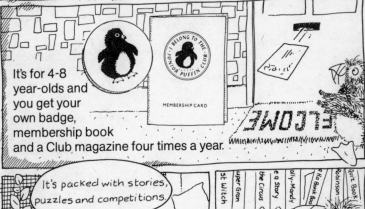

It's for 4-8 year-olds and you get your own badge, membership book and a Club magazine four times a year.

It's packed with stories, puzzles and competitions.

You get a chance to buy new books!

And there's lots more! For further details and an application form send a stamped, addressed envelope to:

The Junior Puffin Club,
P. O. Box 21,
Cranleigh,
Surrey,
GU6 8UZ